EXPLORE
my world

Clouds

Marfé Ferguson Delano

NATIONAL
GEOGRAPHIC
KiDS

WASHINGTON, D.C.

Look up! Clouds!

They float in the sky above lakes and seas, gracefully billowing in the breeze.

Clouds dapple the skies above country lanes and city streets.

They drift over and under high mountain peaks.

When can you see clouds?
Almost every day. You can
see them in the morning
and in the afternoon.

You can see them
at sunrise and sunset,
glowing golden pink or rosy
red, purple, orange, or blue.

Peekaboo!

You can even see clouds at night, playing hide-and-seek with the moon and stars.

Cloud Collection

What are clouds made of? Water! They are made of millions of very tiny water droplets or bits of frozen water, called ice crystals, that float together in the sky.

Raindrops are made of water droplets. Have you ever tried catching raindrops on your tongue?

The long white trail left behind by a jet is also a kind of cloud. It's called a contrail.

Clouds come in many different sizes and shapes. Here are the three main kinds.

Cirrus clouds look like wispy white brushstrokes.

1

Stratus clouds look like fuzzy gray blankets stretched across the sky.

2

Cumulus clouds look like fluffy balls of cotton.

3

Drip, drop!

Clouds bring the rain that all plants and animals need to live. Flowers and frogs, trees and tigers all need rain.

Rain happens when the water droplets in a cloud bump into each other and stick together. When they become too heavy to float in the sky, they fall down to earth as raindrops.

When it's cold enough, clouds can bring snow!

Snow starts out as ice crystals in a cloud. As the crystals fall through the sky, they stick together and make snowflakes.

One kind of cloud piles up high in the sky, towering like a giant castle. These clouds create storms with pouring rain, wild winds, lightning, and thunder.

Flash, crash, boom!

These are cumulonimbus clouds, also called thunderheads.

Can you say cumulonimbus (kyoom-yuh-loh-NIM-bus)?

If you were an eagle, you could fly through a cloud and feel wetness on your feathers.

But you don't have to fly to feel a cloud. You can walk through one kind. It's called fog. Fog hangs low over land or water.

Cool Clouds

Whether you're on the ground looking up at clouds, or in an airplane looking down at them, clouds are fascinating to watch. Here are some mysterious-looking clouds from around the world.

These bubble-shaped clouds sometimes hang from storm clouds.

Saucer-shaped clouds like this one usually form near mountains.

Why can't we see the top of this mountain?

The rainbow-colored patch in this cloud is called an iridescence.

What colors do you see in this cloud?

Can you say iridescence (eer-uh-DES-ince)?

Sometimes light passing through clouds forms a glowing circle around the moon, called a moon dog.

The Morning Glory is an enormous roll-like cloud that only forms over Australia.

23

When high winds blow, clouds sweep swiftly through the sky, changing shape as they go.

Other times, clouds seem as still as statues. But if you keep looking, you'll see them change shape. Clouds are always moving and changing.

If you could look at Earth from space, you would see that there are always clouds floating somewhere over our planet.

During the day, clouds block the sun's heat, helping Earth stay cool. At night, clouds act like a blanket, helping Earth stay warm.

Thanks, clouds!

Clouds bring us the rain we need to live. They fill the sky above us with beauty. How boring the sky would be without them!

Be a Cloud-Watcher!

Anyone can be a cloud-watcher. All you have to do is look up!

Can you draw some of the cloud shapes you see?

Never look directly at the sun. It can hurt your eyes.

Lie on your back, get comfortable, and gaze at the sky.

Be patient. Take the time to really watch.

Look for big clouds, little clouds, fat clouds, and skinny clouds.

Notice if clouds are moving fast or slow.

What Do You See?

If you watch clouds closely, you can see all kinds of things in them. What shapes do you see in these cloud pictures?

For my soul sister, Makda Kibour
—MFD

Editor: Ariane Szu-Tu
Art Director: Amanda Larsen
Designer: Callie Broaddus
Photography Editor: Lori Epstein
Design Production Assistant: Allie Allen

National Geographic supports K-12 educators with
ELA Common Core Resources. Visit www.natgeoed.org
/commoncore for more information.

Trade paperback ISBN: 978-1-4263-1879-5
Reinforced library binding ISBN: 978-1-4263-1880-1

The publisher gratefully acknowledges Jack Williams, fellow of
the American Meteorological Society, and early education expert
Catherine Hughes for their expert review of the book.

PHOTOGRAPHY CREDITS
*GI: Getty Images; SS: Shutterstock; MP: Minden Pictures;
iS: iStockphoto*
Cover, Erkki Makkonen/E+/GI; Back cover, Jeff Schultes/SS; 1, Nicolas
Raymond/SS; 2–3, Jane Rix/SS; 4–5, SuperStock; 6 (UP), Terry Vine/
The Image Bank/GI; 6 (LO), AJYI/SS; 7, Jarno Gonzalez Zarraonandia/
SS; 8, Patrick Smith/Visuals Unlimited/GI; 9 (UP), Digital Stock; 9 (LO),
Pavelk/SS; 10 (LO), Nutexzles/Flickr Select/GI; 11, M. Pellinni/SS; 12
(UP), Konrad Wothe/MP; 12 (LO), dreamnikon/SS; 12–13, Kolopach/
SS; 13 (UP), EyeWire Images; 13 (LOLE), PeterPhoto123/SS; 13
(LORT), kredo/SS; 14 (UP), Dmitry Naumov/SS; 14 (LO), kzww/SS;
15, Michael Durham/MP; 16, Steve Gettle/MP; 17 (UPLE), Kichigin/
SS; 17 (CTR LE), Kichigin/SS; 17 (LOLE), Kichigin/SS; 17 (RT), Jan
Vermeer/MP; 18 (LE), ANATOL/SS; 18 (RT), Varina Patel/iS; 19, Piotr
Krzeslak/SS; 20, Didier Kobi/Flickr RF/GI; 21, visceralimage/SS; 22
(UP), Jim Brandenburg/MP; 22 (LO), Tamara Kulikova/SS; 23 (UP), Yva
Momatiuk & John Eastcott/MP; 23 (LOLE), Atte Kallio/Flickr RF/GI; 23
(LORT), Donovan Reese/GI; 24, Roy Morsch/Corbis; 25, Wicki58/E+/GI;
26 (UP), Petr84/SS; 27, Mikael Damkier/SS; 28–29, Charles Gurche;
30, Spike Mafford/The Image Bank/GI; 31 (UPLE), paul weston/Alamy;
31 (UP CTR), KuderM/iS; 31 (UPRT), Hanquan Chen/iS/GI; 31 (LOLE),
Stuart McCall/Photographer's Choice/GI; 31 (LORT), John White
Photos/Moment Open/GI; 32, Jeff Schultes/SS; (cloud background),
kredo/SS; (water drops background), Maria Ferencova/SS

Printed in the United States of America
15/WOR/1